Cherokee Rose

poems by

Miriam Moore-Keish

Finishing Line Press
Georgetown, Kentucky

Cherokee Rose

Copyright © 2021 by Miriam Moore-Keish
ISBN 978-1-64662-500-0 First Edition
All rights reserved under International and Pan-American Copyright Conventions. No part of this book may be reproduced in any manner whatsoever without written permission from the publisher, except in the case of brief quotations embodied in critical articles and reviews.

ACKNOWLEDGMENTS

Thank you to my family who, consciously or unconsciously, supported me and inspired these poems. I am proud of y'all.

My deepest gratitude to the following magazines, journals, anthologies, and organizations for first publishing the following in different iterations:

Penultimate Peanut Literary Magazine: "Cherokee Rose"
The Remington Review: "Say that Once There was Laughter" and "The Sixth Grade Girls' Bathroom at 8:22 AM"
Underground Journal: "Outside a House Trying not to be Empty," "Brine," and "Great Blue Heron"
Poets.org: "My Oma Says it is Sacrilege to Drink Wine Cold"
Hoxie Gorge Review: "Espalda Mojada"
The Dead Mule School of Southern Literature: "Two Costumes," "Reconstructed Bridge," and "Hightower Lake in Spring"
Samfiftyfour Literary: "Peachtree"

Publisher: Leah Huete de Maines
Editor: Christen Kincaid
Cover Art: Coco Banks
Author Photo: Erika Spadavecchia
Cover Design: Pono Asunción

Order online: www.finishinglinepress.com
        also available on amazon.com

Author inquiries and mail orders:
Finishing Line Press
PO Box 1626
Georgetown, Kentucky 40324
USA

Table of Contents

Brine 1

Cherokee Rose 2

My Oma Says it is Sacrilege to Drink Wine Cold 3

Espalda Mojada 4

Building Churches 5

Say That Once There was Laughter 6

Hightower Lake in Spring 7

The Sixth Grade Girls' Bathroom at 8:22 AM 9

Biscuit 10

Sacred Harp 11

Pigeons and Doves 12

Great Blue Heron 13

Code Red 14

Mary Mac's 15

Outside a House Trying Not to be Empty 16

Peachtree 17

Reconstructed Bridge 19

Picadillo and Princess Jasmine 20

Warwick 21

Pooh Sticks 22

Two Costumes 23

I am Thinking of Things to Tell my Grandchildren 25

Georgian German 26

Imagined Gardens 28

For "Raisin"

Brine

The fortune teller miracle fish
I bought on the boardwalk must have
felt at home in my oceancrusted palm

that summer when it told me I was fickle
and all I knew about the word fickle
was that it rhymed with pickle

so I thought fickle was like the brine
turning cucumbers to pickles and
my palm to the sea and peanuts
to boiled peanuts to home.

My father mailed me a can of boiled
peanuts when I left the South and said
don't forget where you come from and
I said this is not my heritage this is a can.

I told an old Midwestern man that
they sell boiled peanuts in cans if he
ever wanted to try them but I said

the real way is at a gas station that
you almost miss because of the sharp
turns around the mountains and
the hand painted cardboard sign
advertising regular boiled peanuts
and Cajun peanuts for the adventurous.

I told him that they double bag the peanuts
so you can put the shells somewhere
and he looked into the air behind my
head and thought of somewhere

and he said "I saved a life today.
Maybe more."

Cherokee Rose

My great, great, more greats, grandmother
buried the family silver in the pig sty
and pushed the surrey into the woods
when Sherman's army came through.
She watched the flames tickle the sky,
staining clouds to fire and blackness.

My mother says she was
a strong, independent woman.

My father's stepmother is related to Sherman
and he asks her not to say that so loudly
in public and out to dinner because
people slow motion around,
eyes like the fire of my
ancestors' burning plantations.

My great-grandfather wrote letters to his
"Preciosísima," my bisabuela, from his
Havana sala to her Georgia front porch while
a woman named Elmena cooked his supper.

There is a Confederate monument
a mile from my front door but all I remember
from third grade Georgia history is that
the state flower is a Cherokee Rose.

My Oma Says it is Sacrilege to Drink Wine Cold

My Oma wears clothes that
fall like fitted sheets on a laundry
line and hang off her in waterfalls,
her voice falling in rivers

when she says "I'm a tenor"
but really she doesn't have
enough breath to beat gravity
and her voice digs into earth

like my toes while I watch her
rake leaves in our American home.
The leaves don't fall as much in Germany.

My Oma and her husband fell.
They fell out of love together
as origami shapes, folded but
opening in petals to see pollinated
wounds and flesh inside.

She drinks Glühwein heated on the stove.
I imagine it steamstains the air bloody
and I imagine what would happen if
Jesus could turn saltwater to wine,
how it would stain the tablecloth
when she cries while we sing the blessing.

Espalda Mojada

was a word I first learned
on a vocabulary list in
eleventh grade Spanish class,

the Times New Roman font
carving backbones into phonemes,
forcing English-speaking eyes
to halt their tongues at the top
of their hard palates

instead of tasting the fresh air
between teeth, the freedom in
the cold sensation of *th*.

Espaltha:
dripping the word off the lips,
a leaking faucet that hasn't
yet decided if it should
turn into a stream, maybe a river—

like rivers between shoulder blades,
eroding the back with rain and sweat
on Atlanta mornings,

walking to school
carrying a backpack
full of new words.

Building Churches

They're building newer churches
out of wood these days.

Maybe they ran out of stone
or maybe there's only enough
money in the collection plate for trees.

Some churches I see
living on access roads
are made out of something else.
I don't know what. Plastic, maybe.

Plastic like the rosary a nun
gave me so I could count my prayers
in infinite circles and
wear down my fingerprints with wishes,

my fingers turning to sea glass,
beaten against rocks

like the ones they used to cut up,
building homes for their prayers.

Say That Once There was Laughter

There is a book of poems my family
would read at the dinner table.

It sits full of drawings and funny quotes
on the shelf where we put
Saturday morning biscuits,

creased on favorite memorized pages,
the binding worn down to
the funniest parts featured between
bites of field peas with chow chow,
turnip greens, and fried green tomatoes.

Once we could hardly get down
dinner without laughing it back
onto our plates, smiles frozen
in silent joy shared across cans of
dilly beans and my sister's hot sauce.

When I come back now, we eat in
the dining room that we used to save
for guests and the book is in the other room.

And when we do get it out nowadays,
we laugh out of habit
because it is what we always did.

Hightower Lake in Spring

My family owns a lake house
halfway between Georgia and Alabama
where the clay is still red and the sun
baked it under our nails when we dug
for nightcrawlers, my cousins and I.

My cousins and I caught largemouth bass
and bream for dinner with our nightcrawlers
still squirming against their hooks,
oozing a call to the fish we would eat
with grits and collards, singing
rounds and family songs around the table.

The huckleberries grow a trail leading
to the lake house and my cousins and I
would call them "hucklebabies" and purple
our hands with their juices, licking the
stickysweet to a stain to cup toads in the
lines of our palms on early mornings.

In the late summer the wildflowers
wither and leave their stems like I
left the South and the huckleberries to
a stain. The wildflowers mark the memory
of the wind and scatter across the north
Georgia mountains, toes of the Appalachians.

We scattered, my cousins and I, singing
our new songs and planting our new seeds.
We squirmed against home's hook, pulled like
wildflowers in the wind to new homes.

The lake house is quiet now, the birds and frogs
keeping time, filling the air. But there is still a
picture of my cousins and me jumping off the dock,
arms outstretched, toes pointed, and every cell

reaching for the water even though the frame is covered in pollen from spring and there are no hucklebabies this time of year.

The Sixth Grade Girls' Bathroom at 8:22 AM

We faced the crowd in the mirror,
the dirt-cracked reflection in front of the
sink that had fallen off the wall the
year before, so more of us could apply

the eyeliner our parents wouldn't
let us wear when leaving the house before
blowing southern humidity out of our
hair with automatic hand dryers after
our walk to school with unlined eyes,

becoming women in the reflections
in front of us, darkened by lowered
taxes and public school fluorescence
reflected in eyes too bright to be so tired.

Biscuit

Six tablespoons of shortening is all I remember
from my mother's Saturday morning biscuit recipe
that I suppose also works on other days
but we never made them on non-Saturday days
so no one can say for sure.

She let me measure the six tablespoons,
calf buried to thigh, knees hugging the bowl,
the queen of the countertop, shortening branding
oil on skin, a fingerprint smeared on the faucet
we never thought to clean.

She let me make faces out of the dough:
eyes, noses, mouths instead of biscuit lumpshapes,
steaming the plate under applesauce hair and
a grits beard (with flecks of bacon on weeks
we didn't buy sausage for the sausage ears).

You don't really write about home until you leave it,
I find, and maybe it is a finding on its own,
a hide and seek or a Hansel and Gretel dropping
biscuit crumbs all the way to the front door
that rattles in its frame when the train comes by.

Sacred Harp

I heard some people
singing Sacred Harp songs
yesterday but they were
different tunes to
the ones my family sings
at Thanksgiving but the
words were still
on Jordan's banks and
the promised land was
still there, it was
just transposed.

Pigeons and Doves

My dad had two homing pigeons
in Germany named "Engel" and "Teufel"
and whenever he let them out
and waited for them to fly home to him,

they would fly back to the man who
sold them, back to their first home.

When I got confirmed in church
(fourteen years old too young to know
anything of Engels and Teufels,

answering "I will" and "I do"
to the right questions, as taught),

my mother gave me a dove necklace and
told me I always had a home in the church.

I never wore the necklace again
but I did get a tattoo of pigeons
when I was twenty-one

because even though I hear people
scoff that they are rats that learned to fly,

I think a rodent that can exist underneath,
on, and above the earth is an impressive feat,

and I could never tell the difference
between pigeons and doves anyway.

Great Blue Heron

We always kept our eyes pulled by
hairs, feather-lengths above the water
because that is where my grandfather
said the great blue heron sweeps.

Careful or you might mistake him
for his reflection, smooth as the
water before hurricane season,
a twin he whispers to when he is
close enough but who drips into silence
when he lands on the old oaks by
rhododendron and huckleberry bushes.

We would look for the heron, point
wet lake fingers—pruned throughout the
family reunions, hidden from grandmothers
and great-aunts—watch the heron until
its reflection disappeared from the
water around us, bubbling and churning.
The heron twin must have had a hard
time keeping his course.

My great aunt said she wanted to come
back as a great blue heron so now we
squint extra hard, hairs in our pupils
pulled taut to shore. When we go back
my mother watches the herons like she
knows something secret and we all give the
lake one last scan before we drive away.

There are no Appalachian pinky toes outside
my house up here, none cradling the earth,
holding it until sleep. All I see is sky reflected
in puddles from rare yesterday rain.
Now all I have is the great blue.

Code Red

They built apartments
next to the local high school.

I told my sister the cinderblocks
were trees when I was in school.

Kids my parents didn't want
me to befriend smoked
secrets wrapped in paper
turned brown by unwashed hands

and a farmers market with
mayhaw jelly and basement-pickled
okra arrived on weekends

to chase out a week of smoke
with free samples.

The path I used to walk after school
to buy forbidden eyeliner
is a parking deck for hybrid cars
and "coexist" bumper stickers.

My sister told me students are scared
of people shooting from the parking spaces,

from the apartment balconies facing south
to look on the football field

on Friday nights,
spectators in the stands.

Mary Mac's

The sound of breaking
tissue papered fry
painted on okra
overpowered your voice
when we talked about
what we would do

but now when I go back and
sit in the room with
the big windows,
we talk about what we did,
about how I thought potlikker
was pot liquor and I didn't
know if I could order it
if I was under twenty-one

and about the waitress
who gave back rubs
and the time my sister found
a bug in her squash casserole
and the time my Oma filled up
on chicken livers and said it's okay

I'll just sit and wait and listen
until I can eat again.

Outside a House Trying Not to be Empty

I sit outside my house.
It is trying not to be empty
and failing.

A wind chime rings
but I can't tell from where,
absorbed into the air
by osmosis maybe.

A whip-poor-will calls.
I always thought it was a
"whipperwill" but now
I wonder who is Will?
Does he know his pain
is in every song?

I can't tell if the warm
January breeze is the daughter
of Georgia or climate change

but it pushes a fly
onto the page of my book.
He sits on a P but maybe
it is a D. There is a fly
covering it, after all.

And the sun is in my eyes
and poor Will is in my ears.
I think about praying for him
but decide against it, I don't pray,

my mouth a church,
the steeple of my soft palate
echoing songs that worship words.

Peachtree

After prom my friends and I went to the
Krispy Kreme on Ponce, near Peachtree,
a road built by Black convicts in
Old New South slavery, a backbone of
Atlanta named after the plantations.

We licked sheets of sugar off our lips,
wax-like and pinked by the lipstick we wore
to tell ourselves we knew about the world,
to tell the world we thought we knew about
that we could see it clearly under our false lashes.

I remember our eyelids heavy from their weight
or maybe we were just tired.

I don't remember the day after prom
but I'm sure I was sore from high heels, sure
I looked through the pictures of the
previous night, picking out the ones
that made me look older, taller,

the ones that made my eyebrows look smaller
and my hair look straighter, smoother.

Back then small eyebrows were *in* and
my friends told me to straighten my hair
but that didn't stop strangers from touching it.

Anyway, it would curl up as soon as I stepped
outside in Georgia air, unable to ignore its roots.

In prom pictures my friends and I stood in a line,
in a pattern of Black, white, Black, white so no one
could call us racists, *see look I have Black friends*
we could say if anyone asked but they never did.

After school those years my friends and I
would walk downtown and eat ice cream and
sit in the sun, leaning on an obelisk I would learn
years later was a Confederate monument.

I never knew because I never looked up.
I only looked down at the melting ice cream,
trying to catch it before it changed form.

My city removed the obelisk after years
of asking and of the state saying no.
I think they tried to put a fence around it
but that didn't stop strangers from touching it,
spray painting it, hitting it, pushing it,
waging a new war for a *New* New South,
all of us strangers to our roots—or maybe
not as strange as we would like to think.

We non-strangers would drive down Peachtree
every Sunday to a church where people soft and
empty like wax figures looked into nothing—
or maybe it was God—silently wishing to
do justice and walk humbly before clacking
their high heels into a reception hall for free
Krispy Kreme doughnuts before leaving

to beat the traffic and beat the rush and win,
I guess, to go home to their plantation-style houses
encircled by never-ending wraparound porches
sagging from the weight of their age, tired.

Reconstructed Bridge

The stable where I rode horses
had a bridge across a creek where,
leading the horses to the pasture,
we would hold their heads
a little tighter, speak our words
a little softer, and guide their hooves

over planks of wood comforting holes
in the original architecture.

They said the bridge was in the same
place that Sherman's army marched,
that if they came that way now,
the horses would be met with fire,

bleaching their coats with
the sun of the earth, roaring away
their whinnies, the ones they let out
sometimes when they get nervous

crossing the reconstructed bridge
while the rain off a city reinvented
turns to steam on the Chattahoochee.

Picadillo and Princess Jasmine

I dressed up as a "Gypsy" two years in a row
for Halloween when I was three and four.

I spent the night with my friend Gabrielle
the night my sister was born
and my parents were in the hospital.

I showed up the next morning dressed as
Princess Jasmine because Gabrielle
had to be Belle.

When I moved to England,
I cooked my great-grandmother's
picadillo slowly, stirring in the rice,
watching it change color.

Warwick

I learned from a sign that Warwick, Georgia
is the home of the National Grits Festival.

My eyes were grateful for something
to focus on besides the road
shaved down by cotton plantations
with names like *Whispering Pines*
and *Oak Grove* and one called *Liberty*,

all of them choking the road from
both sides, closing in to a point
on the horizon that I would reach

before settling on a new distance,
vanishing point by vanishing point,
connecting the dots to the
Spanish moss line in a world
I used to think was vanishing as well.

Pooh Sticks

My grandfather and I used to play *Pooh Sticks*,
dropping our carefully selected competitors
into tar-like water groaning under the overpass,

pulling itself out of bed to shuffle into slippers,
pour the coffee, and distribute our sticks
on the other side: placing them in the arms
of impatient eyes welcoming our prodigal twigs.

Last night I saw a drunken college student alone
on the Cam, sticks blooming from his fingers,
his feet crying across the cobbles to the other side
of the bridge to search for what he let go, too far
downstream now in the river pregnant with rain.

You and I walked from the field to the woods
to see the stained-glass window sun through
the veins of leaves, laughing with shine.

I saw a stream by the path, consuming its old friend.
I said if it were bigger or if we were smaller
we could play *Pooh Sticks* but we would need
something to cross over: something to cover
the water, something to make it to the other side.

Two Costumes

I.
In kindergarten when we learned about Thanksgiving,
my teacher counted us off one two one two one two
into *Pilgrims* and *Indians* to act out what we thought
was the first Thanksgiving dinner.

I was assigned *Indian*, told to invent an "Indian Name"
for myself ("Indian Names," she said, described your
identity, they meant something, something earned),
told to wear paper feathers in my curls, told to sit
at a table of moccasins, buckled shoes and black hats
one two one two one two one two, and
to pick at squash and sliced turkey deli meat.

I chose to keep the name my parents gave me,
earning the Hebrew word for "rebellion," maybe.

II.
In third grade my school required a unit on
local native tribes, roped off and sanitized
in textbooks and historical markers
(my teacher did love hand sanitizer).

Some people said they loved Disney's *Pocahontas*
and on curriculum night we all dressed in
craft store buckskin fabric dresses,
hot glued by parents, hair braided, feet bare,
to present on the Cherokee and Creek.

We read off index cards by our shoebox
dioramas about the Trail of Tears,
the need to restore and preserve, and we
said "thank you" when neighbors,
other teachers, and family members said,
"you look like such a cute little Indian."

I said "cool" when my friend with the red hair
told me she was related to Pocahontas.

I am Thinking of Things to Tell my Grandchildren

When my grandmother says
that I'm too skinny and feeds me
dessert after every meal, even breakfast,
I start thinking of things
to tell my grandchildren

I will say, "when I was your age
I didn't have one of those
intellectual telephones.
I had a phone that I bought myself
with minutes I bought myself
at the Walmart down the street
that the white folk called
the bad side of town."

I will say things like my mother
is starting to when we walk around
her hometown and she says,
"that church was a fruit stand
when I lived here."

I am thinking of things
to tell my grandchildren
when my grandfather turns from
the football game on TV and asks
"do you think it's that cold in Shreveport
or are people leaving because
they know how the game
is going to end?" and I say

"it must be cold in Shreveport
because people like to see
how things play out even when
they know how they will end."

Georgian German

My Oma on the phone
says *genau* every three words.
Her double chin sways side to side
nodding along with her,
"exactly, exactly."

My other grandmother
pronounces the c and t
in "exactly" a second apart
because she majored in English,
she likes me to remember that.

My grandfather ordered a
baked potater on one of their dates
and it still haunts him:
his Louisiana making
one vowel three,
letters filling the gaps of air
between gums and cheek,
water becoming the
shape of its container.

Drawl trickles down
the back of my throat
and if it is deep enough
I can catch it with a cane pole.
My German is dead before
I pull it out of the water,
exhausted from the fight.

Maybe my German is tired from all
the *gute nachts* my Oma and father
told me before they said *schlaf gut*.
Nighttime was all it got.

From Georgian I got
*I love you punkin', sweetie,
honey pie, biscuit, baby, sugar...*

I only use my German to say
ich liebe dich because love
sounds like unfeeling
and it feels like goodbye and maybe,
just maybe, I'll see you tomorrow.

Imagined Gardens

I think I will have a weed garden, I've told you,
give them a place to be welcome and not plucked up
because they planted themselves and didn't wait
for someone else to give them permission to live.

I also think I will have an herb garden so I can
eat what I've made. I don't know if this is how
it works but it feels powerful, like eating the sun,
and it feels like the circle of life that way—

creating and consuming and bragging about my
creeping thyme that crawls through the cracks
in rocks, putting its arms around fighting brothers
turned to stone, pushing them apart just enough to
remind them how much they miss each other.

I want to go to sleep each night excited for what new
colors and shapes have invented themselves, what new
dishes we will cook with the sun we have captured,

My curls falling in love with the shape of your finger,
ivy falling in love with the space between bricks.

Miriam Moore-Keish is a writer and editor originally from Atlanta, Georgia. She holds a bachelor's degree in English Literature from Macalester College and a master's degree in Children's Literature from the University of Cambridge. Her current projects include developing anti-bias and anti-racist preschool curricula, editing children's books, working for the organization We Need Diverse Books, and drinking large quantities of tea. Miriam explores Southern identity, family, religion, race, and womanhood in work appearing in places such as *Poets.org, The Perch, and the Dead Mule School of Southern Literature*. She once nearly got fired for telling short stories by Edgar Allan Poe to kindergarteners.

www.ingramcontent.com/pod-product-compliance
Lightning Source LLC
LaVergne TN
LVHW041511070426
835507LV00012B/1484